WHEN I WAS 18

Haziba Elahi

Think Tank Books

Title: When I Was 18
Author: Haziba Elahi
Published by: Think Tank Books in 2026
Address: RZ-26/27B, Ashok Park, West Sagarpur, New Delhi - 46
Website: thinktankbooks.com
Email: editorial@thinktankbooks.com

ISBN: 978-93-91607-36-4 / eISBN: 978-93-91607-68-5

Price: INR 220/-
Retail price listed is only for the Indian subcontinent.
Selling price may vary elsewhere.

Contents

Acknowledgement

This book grew from moments of silence and nights filled with questions.

To my family whose love and patience carried me through, thank you for believing in me when I struggled to believe in myself, these pages live because of you. For holding these pages and pieces of my eighteen thank you.

About the Book

When I was 18, is a heartfelt journey through my eighteenth year—a time of firsts, lessons and self discovery. Through poems and reflections I share the struggles, joys and quiet moments that shaped me. It's a story of growth, love, mistakes and the strength found in the family.

This poetry collection is a glimpse into the heart of youth, the courage to face challenges, and the journey of becoming myself. Turn the pages and step into my world.

When I Was 18

When I was 18,
I wanted to set the sky on fire,
run faster than rules,
and laugh louder than silence.
I wore my scars like bandages,
my dreams like weapons,
and every no I heard
just fueled the yes inside me.
Eighteen was not a number
it was a roar.

Fading Childhood

I left my childhood
on the last swing of the park,
its chains still trembling
from a goodbye I never said.
I see it in the toy box,
dusty with years,
that no longer fits in my hands.
The last bell of school
still rings in my chest,
but my uniform hangs quiet,
like a memory outgrown.
At eighteen,
I wave goodbye
to the little me
who still wanted
to believe in forever.

Mistakes and Lessons

At eighteen
I thought I knew the map,
but every turn I took
was a blind guess.
I trusted too quickly,
spoke without listening,
ran after dreams
without tying my own shoes.
Mistakes became heavy stones,
but I carried them long enough
to learn they were not punishments,
they were teachers.
They taught me patience,
they taught me silence,
they taught me that falling
is only half the story.
The other half is rising.
Now, when I look back,
I don't see shame,
I see stepping.

Dreams and Fears

My dreams climb out of me,
louder than homework,
brighter than my failures.
They sit beside me as kings;
why not?
Dreams are like candles,
my fears are winds.
Some nights the flames flicker,
some nights they go dark.
But still,
I keep lighting them,
believing even the smallest glow
can outshine the storm.

Who Will I Become

Will I be the voice I once silenced?
or the silence I once feared?
Who will I become,
when the dust of childhood
has settled on my shoes?
A dreamer with cracked maps,
or a realist with heavy pockets?
Will I still chase the sky
like it owes me an answer,
or will I learn to live quietly
under its endless questions?
At eighteen,
I don't know the shape of my future,
but I know it begins with me.

Running into the Storm

I didn't wait for calm skies,
I ran straight into the storm.
Lightning split the path before me,
rain blurred my vision,
but I kept moving-
the heart loud,
the fear louder.
Every step felt like surrender,
yet every step was survival.
So the storm did not break me-
it revealed me.
When the clouds tore open
and silence returned,
I realized
I had not been chasing it,
I had been chasing myself.

What I Carried with Me

I carried the weight of eighteen.
Dreams that slipped through my hands, mistakes
that
carved shadows on my skin,
and nights when freedom felt louder than
wisdom's quiet voice.
I carried laughter too,
the kind that hides in old photographs,
and the stubborn fire
that made me rebel
just to prove, I was alive.
I carried broken dreams like notebooks scribbled
with
hope and failure,
but inside the torn pages,
I found pieces of
myself
still worth keeping.
I carried fear, courage,
but I carried courage too,
and somewhere between the two
I began to see-
I was never just my pain,
I was the lessons it left behind.

The Mirror I Broke

I shattered the mirror
trying to escape my reflection,
but the shards only multiplied me. A thousand
broken
versions, each asking who I was.
Pain was not the wound,
it was the question, echoing louder than silence:
Will you keep hiding,
or will you finally see?
Cut my hands,
so I gathered the fragments,
bled my truth into the glass,
and in the red shimmer
I saw someone new-
not whole
but honest.

The Ghost of Eighteen

Eighteen lingers,
like perfume on an old scarf, faint,
but impossible to forget.
It whispers of choices, some I wish to erase,
others that built the bones of who I am.
Eighteen is gone,
but it still lives in me
not as a cage,
but as the key
to my tomorrow.

Nights Without Permission

Those nights were not mine to take,
yet I stole them anyway-
slipping past curfews,
chasing laughter,
writing my own freedom in the dark.
The world slept,
reckless, fragile, alive,
but I was awake.
Every stolen hour
was a quiet rebellion,
a lesson etched in moonlight.
Sometimes we find ourselves,
only when no one is watching.

Wrong Turns, Right Lessons

I took roads that bent the wrong way,
chased shadows
thinking they were light.
I trusted maps drawn by others,
only to find myself lost
in places no one warned me about.
Yet every stumble carried a mark,
every detour whispered a truth.
The wrong turns
were never wasted.
They taught me how to read the stars,
how to trust my own compass,
how to walk forward
without fear of being lost again.
In the end,
the mistakes I made
became the milestones
that showed me who I was.

Toys in Dust

They sleep in silence,
tiny kingdoms once alive in my hands-
soldiers without wars,
dolls without names,
cars with no roads to race upon.
I thought I left them behind
to grow into something greater,
but each time I return,
I find myself smaller-
a child hiding in the dust.
Their silence speaks
not of endings,
but of echoes,
reminding me
childhood never disappears,
it only waits
to be remembered.

Shadows and Healing

Shadows drift across my skin,
echoes of battles I've held within.
They rise at dusk, they haunt the day,
yet guide my heart in a quiet way.
For every shadow holds a trace,
of broken time, of a tender place.
Not all darkness is meant to stay,
some shapes of night can light the way.
Healing does not come in haste,
it grows in silence, it will not waste.
Like rivers carving stones apart,
it writes its wisdom across the heart.
The wounds I feared, the scars I hide,
are softened now by the turning tide.
Shadows remain, but they softly bend,
teaching me pain can also mend.
And so I walk, both torn and whole,
with shadows stitched into my soul.
For even in night, the dawn is near,
healing is born where shadows appear.

The Exam That Failed Me

I held my dreams
inside an answer sheet.
Questions stared at me
like strangers I couldn't speak to.
And when the results came,
the red marks
bled louder than my heartbeat.
For a moment,
I thought my future had ended
in the silence of one exam hall,
but later I learned
failure was not the end of my story,
it was the comma that pushed me
to rewrite the sentence.

Rebellion and Freedom

At eighteen,
I wore my silence like chains,
but inside me
thunder was learning its name.
I wasn't breaking rules-
I was breaking out of myself,
peeling away the skins
others stitched into me.
Every 'don't' they threw
became a stepping stone,
every locked door
a secret invitation.
I didn't want to burn the world,
I only wanted air,
a sky wide enough
for my unfinished wings.
Rebellion was never rage-
it was the courage to say,
I belong to myself
and freedom
was the echo
that finally answered back.

Growing Up

I grew up in shadows and sunlight,
with pockets full of broken toys
and a heart full of unfinished dreams.
I mistook freedom for flight,
and mistakes for chains,
yet each fall was a lesson,
each scar, a quiet teacher.
Growing up was not sudden,
not a single moment,
but a slow unfolding-
like petals learning
the courage to meet the sun.

The Horizon Ahead

The horizon is not an ending
but a question stretched across the sky.
It dares me to step forward,
to carry my scars as proof
that I have lived,
that I have fallen,
and still, I rise.
I do not know what waits-
storms or sunlight,
loss or love-
but the horizon does not ask me to know.
It only asks me to believe
that moving forward
is better than standing still.
So I walk,
with trembling steps
and stubborn hope,
toward the horizon ahead-
a future I cannot see,
but one I refuse to stop seeking.

The Wrong Hands

I gave my trust like an open door,
you entered softly, but left me sore.
Your words were sugar, your silence stone,
I learned the hard way I stood alone.
A promise broken, a mirror cracked.
Truth revealed what kindness lacked.
Yet in the ruins, strength was reborn.
The lesson learned- I trust no more.
But scars can guide where love belongs,
I rise rebuilt, my heart more strong.

Through Hardships

The nights were heavy, the day unkind,
a storm kept raging inside my mind.
Dreams collapsed like fragile glass,
hope slipped quietly, hard to grasp.
I carried wounds no eyes could see,
burdens that almost swallowed me.
Yet every fall became my ground
to rise again, more firm, profound.
Hardship carved me
sharp and true,
I found my strength in breaking through.

Their Struggle, My Roots

I saw their hands, rough and worn,
building a life where hope was born.
Silent nights, with dreams on hold,
stories of sacrifice never told.
Every tear they hid away
became my courage, day by day.
They bent so I could learn to stand,
they fought the storms with empty hands.
Their struggle carved the path I take,
their love the fire I'll never break.

One Day

I am ashamed, my steps fell weak,
I could not reach the heights they seek.
Their dreams were stars I could not claim.
and still I bow beneath the shame.
But in this heart a fire stays
to turn regret to brighter days.
I'll build the wings I lacked before,
and knock with pride on their open door.
For though I stumbled, lost and tried,
one day I'll make them glow with pride.

Footprints Beyond Time

Your footsteps faded from the ground,
yet in my heart they still resound.
The paths you walked, the words you gave,
still guide me now, beyond the grave.
Time may steal the breath, the voice,
but not the lessons, not the choice.
You built in me a quiet flame,
that burns each time I say your name.
Though I can't see your gentle face,
your spirit lingers, a soft embrace.
Footprints beyond time, steady and true,
Grandfather, I still walk with you.

Wounds in Wings

I tried to fly with broken skies,
my dreams were heavy, truth disguised.
Each wound I bore became a mark,
a silent flame against the dark.
The pain that tore, the nights I cried,
became the strength I hold inside.
For wings are fragile, yet they heal,
each scar a proof of what is real.
Though storms may tear, I will ascend,
my wounded wings will help me mend.

The Silence I Survived

The silence pressed against my chest,
a weight unseen, an endless test.
No voice came to hear my cries,
only echoes in the night sky.
I spoke in tears no one could read,
a silent scream, a hidden need.
Yet in that hush, I found my flame,
a strength that rose without a name.
For though the quiet nearly drowned me,
I wore survival like a crown.

The Road I Shouldn't Have Taken

I followed a path that wasn't mine,
blind to the warning, deaf to the sign.
Dreams looked brighter, the truth looked dim,
hope was loud, but wisdom was slim.
I stumbled, I faltered, yet still I
walked carrying silence,
where my heart once talked.
Though pain was the toll, I can't regret,
the lessons I carry, I won't forget.
A wrong turn taken, a truth now known,
even lost roads can guide us home.

The Cost of My Silence

I buried my voice in trembling nights,
believing quiet would keep me safe.
But silence carved scars deeper
than any shouted truth could make.
Each word I swallowed became a stone,
pressing heavy on my chest.
I paid in pieces of myself,
broken, unseen, unheard.
The cost was losing who I was-
until courage taught me to speak.

The Hunger of Empty Roads

The roads were hollow, they swallowed
my name,
each step I took felt more like shame.
Dreams lay shattered like glass on the ground,
but silence ruled and made no sound.
They fed on the fire
I tried to hide,
they burned the truths I kept inside.
Yet even in ashes, I refused to fall-
the empty roads had not killed it all.

Bridges I Built from Ashes

From ruins of choices, I began again,
gathering dust where dreams had burned.
The fire that broke me also cleared
a path my feet had never learned.
I stitched together the broken parts,
turned grief into bricks of strength.
Each step was shaky, yet it held,
carrying me across regrets length.
From ashes rose a fragile way,
a bridge to light, where hope could stay.

Pillars Beside Me

When the nights grew heavy and silence was loud,
when I felt too small in a world too proud,
my siblings stood close, never letting me fall.
Their strength was a shelter, their love held it all.
They carried my burdens, they shared my tears,
they lit up my path through the shadowed years.
Not all heroes are strangers we meet in the fight,
some live in our home, holding our light.

Lessons in My Scars

I tripped on roads I thought were mine,
mistook the stars for false design.
I trusted hands that let me fall,
I chased loud dreams, ignoring all.
But every wrong became a guide,
a quiet teacher by my side.
To youth, I say - don't fear the pain,
mistakes are seeds, not wasted rain.
Each scar you earn, each tear you weep,
is a wisdom carved for you to keep.

The Puzzle of Life

Life is a question no mirror can solve,
a dance of mistakes where shadows evolve.
It hides in laughter, it bleeds in pain,
it leaves us broken, yet whole again.
A storm that teaches, a fire that heals,
a book of secrets no lock conceals.
Not every answer is meant to arrive,
but the beauty is simply- being alive.

The Questions That Raised Me

I grew up holding riddles in my chest,
answers hid while doubts confessed.
Why do dreams slip through my hand?
Why do promises turn to sand?
Each question carved me, sharp and deep,
they woke my soul when I should sleep.
Not every answer I could see,
but the questions
they raised me.

Whispers Behind My Back

They spoke in shadows, never
to my face,
turning my silence into a misplaced disgrace.
Every gathering felt like a quiet trial,
their laughter was heavy, their kindness fragile.
They measured my worth in careless words,
as if my dreams were cages for caged birds.
But little they knew, their whispers
fed the fire inside me that burned instead.
I learned that voices cannot define
the path I carved,
the heart that's mine.
So let them murmur, let judgment stack,
I rise beyond the
whispers behind my back.

Rooms I Cry In

There are rooms no one has entered,
walls that know my
voice too well.
They keep the secrets of my breaking,
each echo a story I never tell.
The curtains breathe with quiet sorrow,
floors remember my
trembling knees.
I leave my pain pressed in their corners,
like shadows folded with memories.
Yet even in those haunted chambers,
my tears became rivers that mend.
For the rooms I cry in remind me,
every ending can learn to bend.

Stepping Into Nineteen

Eighteen taught me how to fall,
to rise again, to stand tall.
It gave me tears, it gave me fire,
shaped my heart - grew my desire.
Now nineteen opens a brand-new door,
with wiser steps than before.
I carry strength, I carry grace,
a braver soul in a changing place.
The past is written, the future unseen,
but hope walks with me-
at nineteen.

Author's Note

I wrote this book when I was 18—an age where everything felt louder, heavier and more fragile all at once. These words were born from late nights, unanswered questions and moments I thought I would never survive. At the time, writing was not just an expression but my way of breathing through the silence. Every page carries the truth of who I was, what I felt and what I carried with me.

If you are holding this book now, know that it is more than poems, it is a piece of my heart from a younger self who wanted to be heard.

If even one sentence stays with you, then these pages have truly done their work. A little of my roads is now ours—thank you.

- Haziba